THE FACTS OF

CRAPS

**Experiencing the Thrill of
Casino Dice Action**

WALTER I. NOLAN

CASINO PRESS • NEW YORK

THE FACTS OF CRAPS

Copyright © 1984 by Casino Press, Inc.

All rights reserved.

ISBN: 87019-013-X

10   9   8   7   6   5   4   3   2   1

This book was produced for the publisher by RAY FREIMAN & COMPANY

CONTENTS

A complete list of
THE WORLD'S FINEST LIBRARY OF GAMING BOOKS
can be found on pages 111-112

PREFACE

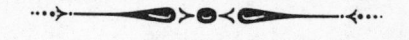

America's casino resorts offer a variety of games of chance, each with its own appeal and action. The Craps table is where you'll find the action at its most exciting, as people respond to the age-old lure of betting the dice. Here you'll find everyday vacationers and high rollers alike caught up in the suspense of a roll, bets placed according to the odds and returns possible or maybe just placed on a hunch.

At the Craps table everyone, high roller as well as beginner, plays against the house, and each can play his own strategy or system. They can even play at the same table, although the beginner will be wise not to fall under any psychological pressure to imitate the person who has large sums of money he is willing to risk.

Craps, like the other casino games, has a built-in house advantage. There are players who emerge big winners, but when things are averaged out, the players lose more than they win. So the better objective with play is enjoyment of the action offered. This guide will introduce you to the enjoyment of Craps, teaching you how to play the game and how to gamble intelligently so as to achieve the most entertainment for the least amount of money . . . and you get a chance at winning.

Play for fun! The game of Craps is easily learned; *The Facts of Craps* will help you become a confident player, showing you how to minimize risk of loss and play for the best chance of a win. Join the more than 2 million people who have found our Casino Press Fact Books a reliable introduction to the casino's games of chance, allowing maximum enjoyment of the play opportunities offered by clarifying available strategy choices.

1

CRAPS—WHAT IS IT?

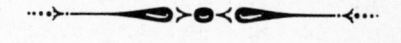

Craps, played with dice, is the most exciting game offered by gambling casinos. A blind man can find a Craps table in a crowded casino merely by listening for the raucous comments and cheers being shouted by a Craps game's participants. To a stranger who is visiting a casino for the first time, it must seem strange that this one game, with people standing around a large table, is so outstandingly noisy compared to Roulette and Blackjack, which are games where players sit stone faced in silence, occasionally moving their hands to place chips down or pick chips up.

The reasons for these loud bursts of noise at Craps tables are very understandable once you realize that one mini-second roll of the dice can produce hundreds and sometimes thousands of dollars in winnings for the players as a group, and sometimes one roll will produce these same amounts in losses. A large winning roll sponsors loud cheers for the same reason a winning hit sets off the home-town rooters at a ball game. Naturally large losing rolls bring moans. Other casino games, which are more individualized in their outcomes, rarely produce sequences of mass winnings.

SOME BACKGROUND

The origin of Craps is unknown. What is known is that prehistoric man played games with a six-sided bone that came from the ankle of a sheep. This was the first die. (*Die* is the correct singular for *dice*.) Dice have been found in the ruins of Pompei, in the tombs of Egypt, in ancient excavations in England. They have been made from wood, bone, clay, and of course, ivory. The dice used in modern casinos are composed of cellulose nitrate.

The earliest written record of dice-related mathematical problems or probabilities comes to us from the sixteenth-century Italian physician and mathematician Gerolamo Cardano. The earliest record of any game close to Craps appeared in the eighteenth century in English books about games. The game was called "Hazard" and was pretty much the same as Craps, except that the caster, as the shooter was referred to then, had some options that made things more complicated. By the time Hazard reached this country, it had evolved into the Craps game we play today.

12

WHAT IS IT?

In the eighteenth-century Hazards game, the numbers 2, 3, and 12 were known as "crabs." That's where the name of the current game came from. *Craps* is simply a corruption of *crabs*. Craps entered this country at the port of New Orleans and quickly became popular along the Mississippi, replacing Faro as the main game of chance.

Up until the turn of the century, Craps was conducted as a private game. When efforts were made to "bank" the game—that is introduce one-way house action, as in a casino—it was necessary to charge a 5 percent commission for Don't Pass bets, as these had the advantage over Pass bets. That provided the house percentage. But in the early 1900s, a variation on dicemaker John Winn's "Philadelphia layout" let the bettor make a Don't Pass bet without the 5 percent vigorish by barring the Ace-Deuce. This meant a standoff to the Don't bettor on the Come-Out roll. It was later modified by casinos to the Bar-12 or Bar-2 position we know today. This evolution in providing a house advantage was responsible for taking the game out of the back alleys, and today Craps is the fastest, most exciting game in our casinos.

THE BASIC GAME

Craps is really quite simple as a game. If you've never seen a pair of dice you can still be as good at shooting Craps as anyone in ten minutes.

WHAT IS IT?

Or if at any time in your life you have shot Craps, you already know the basic casino game. Casino Bank Craps differs from the army-style or home-variety game only in the way the payoffs are conducted. The difference is that the casino banks all bets. In the informal game, all players play among themselves and cover or fade each other's wagers. In Bank Craps, when you lose, the casino collects your bet; when you win, the casino pays you. The basic rules that govern who shoots the dice, when his turn to shoot has ended, and who will be the next shooter are exactly the same for both games.

The basic game, whether in private play or in the casino, has the shooter making a bet *before* he makes the first roll of the dice. This first roll is referred to as "coming out." If with this first roll the shooter throws a "Natural" (a 7 or an 11), he wins his bet, and he then makes a new bet and begins again with a new coming-out roll. If, on the other hand, on his first roll he rolls a Crap (a 2, 3, or 12), he loses his bet, but does not "lose the dice." He is free to make another bet and to try again. If on the first roll he throws neither a Natural nor a Crap, he establishes a "point"—a 4, a 5, a 6, an 8, a 9, or a 10. Following his establishing a point he will continue to roll the dice until he either rolls his point or a 7. If he rolls his point before rolling a 7, he wins his bet, "keeps the dice," makes a new bet, and comes out with a new first roll. If, after establishing his point he should roll a 7 before rolling his point, he will lose his bet and he loses the dice, passing them to the person to his left, who then makes a bet and comes out with a first roll of the dice.

If, after establishing a point on the first roll the roller throws an 11 or a Crap on any of the following rolls, the 11 or the Crap would have no effect on either his winning or losing his bet. The winning or losing of his bet, after a point has been established, depends entirely upon the rolling of the point or the rolling of a 7, whichever comes first.

In the private game it is the amount of money the shooter wishes to bet that determines the total amount the other participants combined can bet, with the first person to the right of the shooter having the first opportunity to bet against the shooter. This person can cover (fade) the shooter's entire bet, fade only part of it, or not fade any of it. The privilege of betting against any amount left after a person has faded passes to the person on his right, and so on until the entire bet has been faded. If any portion of the shooter's bet has not been faded, it is returned to him before he makes his coming-out roll.

In the casino game the shooter's bet is faded by the house. Consequently, all the players can bet with the shooter or they can bet against him. The casino banks all the bets. However, the privilege of betting is not unlimited. The casino sets limits on the amount a player can bet. One casino in Las Vegas permits a minimum bet of 25¢ and a maximum bet of $5000 at the same table. Some nearby casinos have limits of a $1 minimum and $500 maximum. Some casinos range from $2 to $2000; others have minimums of $5 with $2000 maximums. The maximum or minimum limit applies only to one particular bet, and since a casino Craps table offers many different bets, a player could have many maximum- or minimum-limit bets working at the same time.

Having the casino bank all bets permits the player to bet in any way he wishes. His direction of bet has not been predetermined for him. The shooter also has this privilege. He can bet that he won't Pass instead of that he will, and if he does this, the other players can still bet he will make a winning roll even though *he* is betting that he won't. As a result of this, the shooter's only function in the casino game, as far as the other players are concerned, is to roll the dice.

It is this free choice of dice direction and all the other bets the casino table offers that make Casino Bank Craps the popular game it is. Once a person has graduated to the casino game he finds the home-style fading game very dull by comparison. However, a person who learns his Craps on the casino table should be aware of the differences between it and the non-casino fading game so, should he ever get involved in such a game, he can protect himself from its pitfalls.

2

THE SETTING

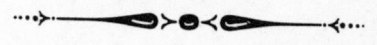

To anyone unfamiliar with Craps, the most confusing thing about it is the setting—the elaborate table with the complicated numbered cloth, the Stickman yelling, the players yelling, and the dealers frantically moving chips (called checks in the casino) all around the table. That's the scene at every busy Craps table and represents confusion and utter chaos to the uninitiated. Despite all that, the game is simple enough so that with just the information and instruction in this book any beginner can soon conduct sophisticated play in a confident manner.

TABLE LAYOUT

The covering on the Craps table is called a layout, and it functions as something of a road map. The layout actually has nothing to do with the play

17

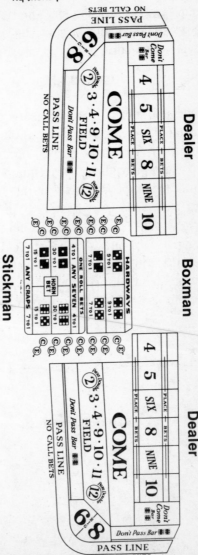

Typical Craps layout. There may be slight variations from casino to casino, but this layout accurately summarizes all the options you will find on any casino Craps table.

of the game as such. Its only function is to keep a complete and accurate record of the bets.

All the lines and different numbers confuse and frighten people. They make a game that is simple and easy to learn look complicated. The layout isn't even necessary to the game; it could be discarded—thrown away—and the game played without it. But this would require all the players and the dealers to remember all the bets and who owns which bet, and confusion would result. So the layout is there for convenience, making record-keeping simpler for player and casino alike.

Each player around the table has places indicated for him on the layout in which his bets are positioned by himself or the house, depending on the type of bet. The player makes bets on the Pass Line, the Don't Pass Line, and takes or lays Odds on those bets as well as on the Field, Come bets, and Big 6 or 8 by putting the bet directly on the layout. All other bets are positioned by the dealers. Once you become familiar with the casino memory system of putting bets on the layout, it's an easy matter to remember, locate, and keep track of your various wagers.

THE CREW

The staff that works at the table is called the crew and generally consists of four men (sometimes women). Their shift lasts eight hours, and this is broken into twenty-minute periods. The staff is made up generally of a Stickman, two dealers, and a Boxman (or two). Each dealer, in turn, works twenty minutes on the stick, calling the dice and running the game. He then moves to a base—there are two, one at each half of the table—where he deals for forty minutes; then he takes a twenty-minute rest period and back to the stick, etc.

At any given time, three members of the crew are working and one is resting. This procedure of a twenty-minute rest every hour is followed in order to keep the crew mentally sharp. Working conditions are difficult. Noise, constant activity, constantly standing in one position, and at times having to deal with impatient or abusive members of the public can be a problem.

The Stickman

The person who directs and conducts the game is called the Stickman. He controls the dice with a curved stick. He also announces the results of each roll of the dice for the shooter, the players, and the dealers, employing a constant and sometimes colorful banter. On hearing the Stickman's call, the dealers pay all winning bets and collect all losing bets.

The Stickman controls the tempo of the game—fast enough to maintain the players' interest and yet at a pace that won't run over the less experienced player. He also acts partly as an auctioneer, announcing the many side (proposition) bets that can be made. Generally, these are bets that are most advantageous to the house and least advantageous to the player.

The Dealers

These two personnel are opposite the Stickman on the "house" side of the Craps table. With the exception of the proposition bets in the center of the layout, the left half of the table repeats itself in the betting spots on the right. Each dealer controls the bets on his "numbers" according to instructions from the bettors or by way of the Come bet (more about that later). The dealer also places the "buck" (sometimes called a "puck"), which is the marker indicating the line point number (if any) of the current shooter.

The dealers have to be extremely sharp and adept at handling and paying off the bets at various odds and denominations. Their arithmetic must be flawless. Good dealers learn the betting styles of their players and anticipate most of their players' betting moves after a few rounds of play. Sometimes they even point out a deviation in the pattern of play on the part of a player, and more often than not they are correct in pointing out that the player forgot to make his usual bet.

The Boxman

The Boxman sits at the middle of the table between the two dealers and is in charge of running the game. He oversees all operations and transactions. He also places the cash in the money slot and examines the dice in play. He makes most decisions concerning any controversies that may arise. If the "claim" is of serious consequence, the floorman or "pit boss" over several tables may overrule the Boxman and act as the final arbiter over a disputed situation. In big games frequented by high rollers, with lots of money in action, you may find two boxmen overseeing the busy action.

THE PLAYERS

Most players are people just like you and me. They yell and gyrate simply because they are playing for amusement and, win or lose, find the game fun. An oft-quoted statement usually attributed to Nick the Greek but actually first voiced by the French statesman Talleyrand goes, "The best thing in life is to gamble and win. The second best thing is to gamble and loss." (Nicholas "Nick the Greek" Dandolos is one of the gambling world's legendary figures.)

Craps as played in the casino is not a group game, and one player's actions in no way affect the other players. All players act individually, making their own bets and then collecting or losing on them according to the results of the dice. The number of players is limited only by the number for which there is space at the table. So if a game looks interesting and you can get to the rail of the table, go ahead and join in. This is the atmosphere of Casino Bank Craps, one of informality and cama-raderie—everyone against the house, even though often no two people will be betting alike.

THE DICE

A pair of dice is made up of two marked cubes identical in size, color, and in the positions of their markings. It would really make no difference to the results of dice games if the dice were different in size or in color or in the relative positions of their markings. As long as each die was a perfect cube and had a different number (1 through 6) repre-sented on each of its six sides, the two cubes would function in relation to each other the same as if they were identical. However, different sizes, colors, and markings would inevitably produce accusations of "loaded dice."

Loaded dice are dice that have weighted sides in order to favor the production of certain numbers. Loaded dice are usually opaque (commonly ivory), with rounded corners that make it easier for them to fall influenced by their weighted sides.

Dice used in casinos have sharp corners. They are transparent and precisely balanced so that no one side is favored, and they are marked in the conventional manner. If the face toward the ob-server is 5, the top of the cube will be 6, and the vertical face to the right will be 3. The face on the opposite side from 5 will be 2. The opposite to 6 will be 1, and the face opposite to 3 will be 4.

If one die was marked conventionally and the other was marked in any other way, such as having a 2 on the opposite side of 6 instead of a 1, a 4 on the opposite side of 5 instead of 2, and a 1 on the opposite side of 3 instead of 4, the odds of the game of Craps would not be changed. But the "intelligent" remarks and bets that the conventional dice markings promote would be lost, and the Craps addicts would become less "expert."

One of the first things a Craps beginner learns is what the number is on the bottom side of the dice, out of sight, resting on the table surface. For example, if a 7 count is on top of the dice, an identical 7 count is on the bottom of the dice. Opposite each 7 made up of a 6 and a 1 is a 7 made up of a 1 and a 6. Opposite each 7 made up of a 3 and a 4 is a 7 made up of a 4 and a 3. Opposite each 7 made up of a 5 and a 2 is a 7 made up of a 2 and a 5.

THE SETTING

Seven is the only number that duplicates on the opposite side. All the other numbers have complementary numbers on their opposite sides. On any one die the opposite sides add to 7. On a pair of dice the opposite sides add to 14. That is why the opposite side of all 7's are always 7.

Since the opposite of a 1 on a die is 6, the opposite sides of a pair of dice showing 2 must be 12 (two 6's), and the total of the two sides is 14. On the opposite side of two dice adding to 3 is 11. On the opposite sides of all combinations of two dice adding to 4 are 10's. On the opposite sides of all combinations of two dice adding to 5 are 9's, and on the opposite sides of all combinations of two dice adding to 6 are 8's.

These are things the new Craps player learns early, and soon he is urging the dice shooter to "turn them over" when the shooter rolls a number that is supplementary to the one he wants. This is basically trivia, but to the serious Craps addict it often has fantasized importance, and this frequently will prompt him to make a Place bet on the number that is supplementary to the one that has been rolled to Pass.

CRAPS LANGUAGE

Craps has a language with expressions peculiar to itself. These are heard from persons expressing what the dice have just done or what they wish the dice to do. In the private game we often hear someone gleefully shout "Snake eyes!" which, translated into English, means the shooter has just rolled a 2 (two 1's on the dice) on his coming-out roll and the person who yelled has just won his bet against the shooter. "Box cars!" may be yelled in winning a bet when a 12 (two 6's) has just been rolled on the come-out.

The shooter has his own expressions in the private game—such shouts as "Come to Papa!" or "Baby needs a new pair of shoes!", exhortations for a win as he throws the dice. Or he might cry out, "Read 'em and weep!" to announce a winner.

At the casino table the shooter might cry for a 7 or 11 on his come-out roll, and he might call for his point number on his following rolls, but he will never shout, "Read 'em and weep!" to the casino. The only time the casino will weep is when there are no players at its tables. The casino is happy when players are at its tables, regardless of whether some of these players win, because as long as money is being bet, the game's returns, which favor the house, will keep making the casino wealthier.

The Stickman makes most of the Craps conversation at the casino table. It is his job not only to direct the game, but also to sell all the bets offered on the table besides the Pass bet. At an active table the Stickman will keep up a constant patter, letting every player know about all the golden opportunities for instant wealth just missed and all the good chances still available. When the Stickman loudly yells, "Ee-yo!" or "Ee-yo 'leven!" he is telling the table that an 11 has just been rolled and that one or more lucky players had bet it. A good Stickman never misses an opportunity for huckstering the Craps table's wares.

3

THE MATH OF

CRAPS

Here is another case of something being so simple that it seems complicated. The game of Craps is easier to learn to play than any card game. Betting is integral to the play, of course. To understand all the various bets, it is only necessary to know the things that can happen when two dice are rolled, and that is not at all complicated.

DICE COMBINATIONS

Each casino die (in the casino, one die is commonly referred to as "one dice," as this is the more popular usage) is a perfect cube, guaranteed perfect to within $1/10,000$ of an inch. When it is rolled, each of the six sides has an equal chance of being uppermost when the die comes to rest. That means one chance in six that the 3 will turn up, one chance in six that the 5 will turn up, one chance in six that the 2 will turn up, etc. Each side has an equal probability.

When a second die is added to form a pair, each of the dice will show one of six sides uppermost. The combination possibilities are one out of six on the one die multiplied by one out of six on the second die, or one out of thirty-six, that any two given sides will come up at the same time ($1/6 \times 1/6 = 1/36$). If you add a third die, you have a one out of six possibility to multiply by all the combination possibilities that can occur with two dice ($1/6 \times 1/6 \times 1/6 = 1/216$). Each time you add a die, you multiply the resultant combination possibilities by 6.

When the spots showing on the uppermost sides of two dice are added together, the total can be any one of eleven numbers—2 through 12 (2, 3, 4, 5, 6, 7, 8, 9, 10, 11, 12). It is the frequency with which these sums appear that is the basis for the game of Craps. This determines the advantage or disadvantage of a bet and the amount paid by the casino to the players on the various bets made in Bank Craps.

The chart that follows shows graphically how two dice produce thirty-six different roll possibilities. It also shows the chances of appearance for each of the eleven numbers (sums) with any roll of the dice.

36 WAYS

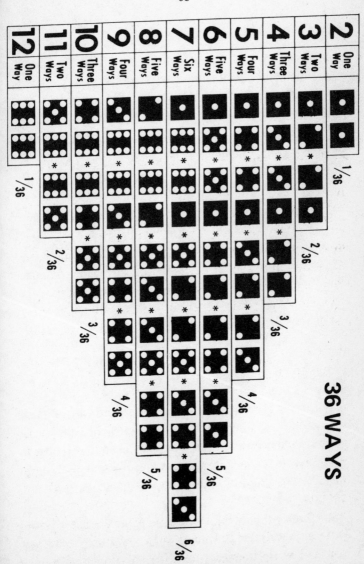

The chance of an event happening lies somewhere between zero (no chance of it happening) and one (a certainty of it happening). With two dice, there are numbers, or events, that can be brought about in a total of thirty-six different ways. The following equation summarizes the various probabilities on each roll. Zero marks the situation before there is any roll—the impossibility of coming up with any combination if you don't roll at all:

$$0 + \frac{1}{36} + \frac{2}{36} + \frac{3}{36} + \frac{4}{36} + \frac{5}{36} + \frac{6}{36}$$
$$+ \frac{5}{36} + \frac{4}{36} + \frac{3}{36} + \frac{2}{36} + \frac{1}{36} = 1$$

Here we've taken the chances of all the numbers and, when added, we find they total 1, a certainty.

In the basic game of Craps we are not concerned with the composition of the numbers. We are concerned only with the sum of the numbers on the two dice. Consequently, we look back to the chart review of the various dice combinations, which total thirty-six, but focus on the chances of obtaining a given sum.

The chart on the next page provides a summary of the possible dice combinations in table form.

	Probability
One way to make a 2	1/36
Two ways to make a 3	2/36
Three ways to make a 4	3/36
Four ways to make a 5	4/36
Five ways to make a 6	5/36
Six ways to make a 7	6/36
Five ways to make an 8	5/36
Four ways to make a 9	4/36
Three ways to make a 10	3/36
Two ways to make an 11	2/36
One way to make a 12	1/36

This chart shows us that each complementary pair of numbers (adding together to 14) has the same probability—2 and 12 (1/36); 3 and 11 (2/36); 4 and 10 (3/36); 5 and 9 (4/36); 6 and 8 (5/36), and 7 and 7 (6/36).

The procedure of making bets, coming out, winning bets and keeping the dice, losing bets and losing the dice, and passing the dice is the same whether betting in a private "fading" game or betting at the casino table, and the odds against the shooter "making a Pass" (throwing a Natural on the first roll or making his point) are the same in both games—1004 to 976 against winning.

It might seem from the odds of 1004 to 976 against the shooter making a Pass that to bet against the Pass would be a certain way of winning, whether in the private game or at the casino. This is technically true for the private game, but it is true only if a player can bet against every shooting decision. In the private game, there are times when the player is the shooter and must bet with the dice, and there are times when a player cannot bet because the shooter's bet has been completely faded before his turn to bet comes around.

In the casino game, betting amounts and directions are not subjected to any controls other than the house limits. Hypothetically, since some casino Craps tables never shut down, someone could always be at the table betting Don't Pass with a certainty of winning over the long run; the casino Craps table could become a source of steady income. The casinos had to have protection against this, so they changed the odds.

The odds of 1004 to 976 *against* making a Pass apply to both the private and casino game. But in the casino game, the odds *against* winning when betting against the shooter making a Pass (that is, a Don't Pass bet) are 976 to 949 rather than 976 to 1004, as they are in the private fading game. This might seem confusing.

If nothing had been changed by the casino to alter the natural odds, the odds for winning by betting Don't Pass would be 1004 to 976 *in favor of* the bettor. Since this would be bad for the house, the casinos specify that when a 12 (or sometimes they specify a 2) is made on the coming-out roll, the bets made to Pass still lose, the same as before, thus leaving the odds at 1004 to 976 against winning on Pass. The bets made on Don't Pass neither win nor lose. Since probability says that a 12 will appear once for each thirty-six rolls, out of the 1980 (1004 losses + 976 wins) coming-out rolls of the dice on which the odds are set, the probable number of 12's will be fifty-five (calculated by dividing 1980 by 36). This makes 949 (calculated by subtracting 55 from 1004) winning rolls for Don't Pass bets, hence the odds of 976 to 949 *against* winning for betting Don't Pass at the casino table.

Before proceeding further we should examine the meaning of several very important terms— *probability*, *odds*, *return*, and *return ratio*—that we will encounter during the remainder of this book.

Probability

The mathematical probability for having something occur is expressed as a ratio—the number of times that this event is likely to happen compared to the total number of ways of which this particular event is a part. For example, we can say that the probability of having two dice add to 2 is once out of thirty-six rolls of the two dice, because out of the thirty-six possible combinations of the two dice, only one of them adds to 2.

Odds

The mathematical odds for having something occur is the ratio of the number of times an event is likely to happen compared to the number of times the event is likely *not* to happen out of the total number of possibilities that exist for either happening. For example, out of the thirty-six possible combinations that a pair of dice can produce, only one combination can add to 2. This leaves thirty-five dice combinations that do not add to 2. Consequently, the odds against a single roll of the dice resulting in a 2 are thirty-five to one (35:1), not thirty-six to one as some people will falsely state.

Return

The return is simply the total amount returned to the bettor after he wins a bet. It is the *sum* of the amount he bet plus the amount he won. For example, should he bet $1 that a 2 will be rolled on the next roll of the dice and be given the correct odds of 35:1, if the 2 is rolled, he would be paid winnings of $35, which when added to his bet of $1 would make a return to him of $36.

The Craps tables do not actually pay 35:1 odds for a bet on 2. Instead, most of them state a payoff of "30 for 1," which means for each $1 bet on a winning 2 there will be a return of $30. Since one of the dollars will be the one that was bet, the odds that the casino is giving are 29:1 not 30:1, which they would like us to believe.

Return Ratio

The return ratio for a bet is the ratio of what the return actually is compared to what it would have been had true odds been given. For example, when $30 is returned for a winning bet on 2 when $36 would be the return at the true odds, the return ratio paid by the casino is $30/36 \times 100 = 83\frac{1}{3}\%$.

Let's compute the return ratios for the basic game of Craps based on the calculated odds of 1004 to 976 against Pass.

When 976 wins are realized and since 976 bets were placed in order to realize these wins, the return is $976 + 976 = 1952$. The total number of bets is $1004 + 976 = 1980$. Therefore, the Pass return ratio is $1952/1980 \times 100 = 98.59\%$, often stated as 98.6% and quite often mistakenly called the "odds for Craps" instead of the return ratio.

THE MATH OF CRAPS

The casino's Don't Pass return ratio is

$$\frac{949 + 949}{976 + 949} \times 100 = 98.59\%.$$

(Remember, the 55 probable 12's are subtracted, as they neither win or lose on Don't Pass.)

What these return ratios of 98.59% mean is that for every $100 bet to Pass or to Don't Pass in Craps, the probability is that $98.59 will be returned, a probable loss of $1.41 for each $100 bet.

Returns and return ratios are what we are interested in when shooting Craps, and so we will refer to these as well as the odds when comparing different bets and methods of betting.

When we observe an average return of $98.59 for each $100 bet, it is puzzling to see some bettors lose so much so quickly at the casino Craps table. Later we will discuss the many bets other than Pass and Don't Pass that a bettor can make at a casino table. We will develop their return ratios and discuss the ways that most losing bettors misplay them. Basically, bettors lose heavily because they do not understand the relationships between probabilities, odds, and returns for their bets.

4

THE PLAY

All players must make their bets before a shooter rolls the dice. The players, even on a come-out roll, are not required to bet "with the shooter" or to bet "against the shooter"—or even to bet at all. There are many betting options on the table. A player can select any of these he wishes. We will discuss them in the order of their importances.

THE PASS LINE

On the outside of the Craps table layout is a narrow enclosure. It runs to the right and to the left of the Stickman along the length of the table and across both ends of the table. This is called the Pass Line, and it is the performance of the bets placed on this line that governs the play on the Craps table. If no bets are placed on the Pass Line, the performance of a theoretical bet placed on it governs the play.

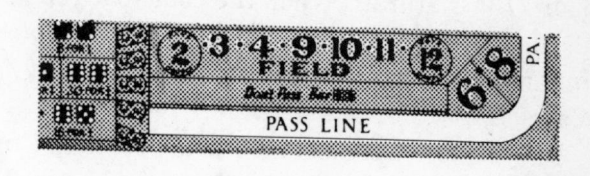

A bet on the Pass Line is a basic-game bet where a 7 or 11 on the first roll wins, a Crap (2, 3, or 12) loses, and any other number establishes a point. Only when a point "sevens-out" does the hand end and are the dice passed to the left.

A bet placed on the Pass Line is called a Pass bet. A win is called a Pass. Thus when we hear that someone had three Passes during his roll, we know he had three winning bets. A Pass bet is an even-money bet, that is, a Pass earns $1 profit for each $1 bet. The Pass bet is made

- before the shooter's first roll,
- before the first roll after a winning decision,
- or after a losing Crap (2, 3, 12) decision.

The bets are placed on the Pass Line by the players themselves directly in front of where they are standing at the table. After all bets have been placed and the shooter has received the dice, the Stickman announces that the dice are "coming out."

Players *win* Pass bets *when the come-out roll is 7 or 11* (a Natural). When the come-out roll is 4, 5, 6, 8, 9, or 10, the number becomes the *shooter's point* and *must be thrown again to win before a 7 is thrown*.

Players *lose* Pass bets *when the come-out roll is 2, 3, or 12* (a Crap) *or when a 7 is rolled before the shooter's point number is repeated*.

Players *pass the dice when a 7 is rolled before the point number is repeated*. (The privilege of shooting the dice passes to the player on the left.) A player does not relinquish the dice if he rolls a Crap on his come-out roll, but shoots again for a new come-out roll.

A shooter may voluntarily pass the dice before completing his hand, and he can do this even before his point has been rolled or the roll has sevened out. In such a case the new shooter is required to complete the point roll started by the player on his right. Should he then seven-out on this point, even though he did not establish it, he would lose the dice and pass the privilege of the roll to the player on his left.

When rolling to repeat a point, rolls of 2, 3, 11, 12, and numbers other than the point and 7 are disregarded. Some other bets made are decided on every roll, but when rolling for a point, only the shooter's point or 7 decide whether the Pass Line wins or loses. Ninety percent of all the action on a Craps table is on the Pass Line. This is where the positive thinkers play.

A player can place a Pass bet *at any time* during a shooter's hand, even after a point is established. This is seldom seen or done, however, and is *not* recommended. The player is facing worse percentages than the come-out Pass bettor, because the player's action was not exposed to the Pass-favorable come-out roll.

Once Pass bets are in action, they may not be removed from the layout until *after* a decision.

Since the Pass bet is the same bet as that of the basic game, its return ratio is also 98.59 percent—an average loss of $1.41 for every $100 you wager.

TAKING ODDS—PASS LINE

When a point number is rolled on the come-out, anyone having a bet on the Pass Line may make an additional bet that the point will be rolled before a 7.

Pass Line Odds

Some casinos allow Single Odds bets, which means you can wager any additional amount *up to* your Pass bet on Odds (sometimes called Free Odds). Some casinos post Double Odds, which means you can additionally wager up to twice your Pass bet. However, this is flexible, and some casinos limiting the Free Odds bet to Single Odds will nevertheless let the bettor exceed his Pass bet in certain instances.

This bet is *the best bet in the casino*, because the house does not have any percentage advantage over the player. The payoff is the correct odds on the point showing, so you get the bet for free— hence the term *Free Odds*. The house doesn't advertise this bet on the Craps layout as there is no position or spot marked for it. It is placed by the player behind his Pass bet *outside* the Pass Line area. (See diagram below.) There can be no spot marked for Odds bets on the table layout because the bet cannot stand alone. An Odds bet can be made only after a point has been established, and the Odds bet is associated only with this particular point.

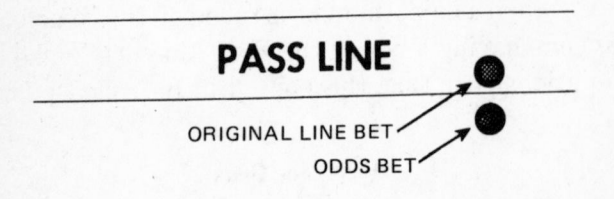

Now, assume you bet $1 on the Pass Line and the shooter rolls a point of 4. If you think he will repeat the point and Pass before sevening-out, you can make an Odds bet by placing $1 as shown above. If the shooter should seven-out, you'll lose both bets. If the shooter should Pass—make his 4 point in this case—the Pass bet would be paid at the normal payoff odds of 1:1, but the Odds bet would be paid the correct odds for the 4 point, or 2:1. So in this case, you would receive $5 in return on a $2 wager, a profit of $3.

The correct Odds bet payoffs for the point numbers are as follows:

- Points *4* or *10*—pay 2:1
- Points *5* or *9*—pay 3:2
- Points *6* or *8*—pay 6:5

You can see that the odds on 5 and 9 and 6 and 8 are such that the correct payoffs would be difficult at $1, and the casino won't make change for less than their minimum bet. Should you make only a $1 bet (at a $1-minimum table) on these numbers, you will only be paid 1:1 on the 5, 9, 6, and 8. However, if your Pass bet was $5, correct payoffs are easily made on the points of 4, 10, 6, and 8, but not on the 5 and 9. If you made a $5 Odds bet on a 5 or 9 point, you would probably only be paid $7 for your $5, thus losing 10 percent of your correct advantage ($3/2$ = $15/10$; $7/5$ = $14/10$; there is $1/10$ or 10 percent of difference). The correct odds would return $7.50 here.

You should bet an *even* amount on the 5 or 9 point. You could bet $4 with a $5 Pass bet, but most casinos giving Single Odds will let you exceed your Pass bet and make an Odds bet of $6 behind a $5 line bet.

The $3 Pass bet is interesting, as a lot of Single odds casinos let you make a $4 Odds bet for a 5 or 9 and a $5 bet for a 6 or 8. However, you should ask the dealer about the house policy first.

All bets in increments of $10 can receive correct odds on *all* the numbers. So at a casino giving Double Odds, a $5 Pass bet permits a $10 Odds bet, which can be paid correctly on all points.

The house percentage is decreased somewhat for the Free Odds player. In the 1980 theoretical rolls that establish the 1004:976 loss-win ratio, in a Single Odds house a Pass player would win 1760 units and lose 1788 units. This means a return ratio of 99.15%, or a house advantage of less than 1%. In a house offering Double Odds, the players would win 2544 units and lose 2572. This means a return ratio of 99.394%, or a house advantage of .606%, only slightly more than one half of 1%. Since the casino doesn't particularly like such low percentages, they'll permit you to remove any Odds bet anytime during a hand before the roll. It can also be made anytime after a point is established. But remember, your original Pass bet must ride to decision.

THE DON'T PASS LINE

This is the opposite of the Pass Line. That is, you bet against the shooter Passing. It pays even money (1:1) when the shooter loses. As with Pass bets, a bet on the Don't Pass is made before the come-out roll. The bet is made directly on the layout in the space provided. If 12 is the bar number, whenever 12 is rolled on the come-out, the bet is a standoff.

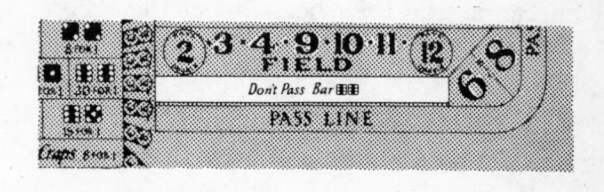

Players *win* Don't Pass bets *when the come-out roll is a Crap 2 or 3* (but not 12) or *when the shooter, after rolling a point number of either 4, 5, 6, 8, 9, or 10, rolls a 7 before repeating the point.*

Players *lose* Don't Pass bets *when the come-out roll is a Natural (7 or 11) or when the come-out roll is a point number that repeats before a roll of 7.*

Although a roll of 12 on the come-out is a losing number for Pass bets, it does not win for the Don't Pass bet. On the Don't Pass bet it only provides a standoff—it neither wins or loses. By doing this, the casino can accept bets on both the Pass Line and the Don't Pass Line and still maintain a slight advantage over the players. *Bar 12* is the term used to cover this facet of Craps, *bar* meaning not allowed. When 2 is barred instead of 12, the results are the same.

Less than 10% of the players bet Don't Pass, possibly because of its association with being pessimistic or negative in approach. One well-known high roller who always made "wrong bets" (Don't Pass) even when *he* was shooting was heard to remark, "I can't stand myself!"

Actually, the bet has almost the identical house advantage as the Pass bet. Out of the theoretical 1980 plays on which the odds are established, the bar-12 Craps will appear 55 times, which leaves 1925 win/loss decisions. Of these, 976 will be Passes and 949 will be Don't Passes (Craps, except the 12, plus miss-outs). So losing 27 units out of 1925 in action, we have $27 \div 1925 = 1.4026\%$ for the house. This opposed to the 1.414% Pass Line disadvantage amounts to less than 12¢ average difference for every $1000 bet.

After the come-out roll and a point number is established, a Don't Pass bet may be retrieved by the player anytime during the shooter's hand. This is *not recommended* play, because *after* sweating out the 8:3 disadvantage (lose on 7, 11; win on 2, 3) of losing on the come-out roll, the Don't Pass bet becomes quite favorable. Out of 1980 theoretical point decisions, the Don't side will lose 804 times and win 1176 times, so Don't Pass will win 372 times more than it will lose, and $372 \div 1980 = 18.78\%$, which is the overall average advantage in the player's favor to leave the bet to decision. Players who retrieve a Don't bet for points of 6 or 8 are giving up a 9.09% advantage. (The table at the end of this chapter summerizes the general return ratio on all bets.)

LAYING ODDS—DON'T PASS

This bet has the same conditions as Pass Line, except the player *lays* the Odds, which is the opposite of *taking* Odds, as on the Pass bets. Conditions are similar in that there are limits in the amount of Odds the player can lay. The player can lay the Odds that will win an amount equal to the original Don't Pass bet. This as with Pass Line Odds, is very flexible. Ask the dealer for assistance in laying Odds. In all cases, you receive *less* than the amount you bet.

The Lay Odds bet is paid at correct odds if . . .

- 4 or 10 is the point, Odds bets are paid 1:2
- 5 or 9 is the point, Odds bets are paid to 2:3
- 6 or 8 is the point, Odds bets are paid 5:6

As the casino has no favorable percentage, Odds on Pass Line and Odds on Don't Pass Line are "free" odds and should be taken advantage of, even when playing the smallest units.

While only 10% of players are "wrong" bettors, it is still surprising that few of these players lay the Odds.

Since most Craps layouts are configured so that the players don't have outside-the-line access for the Odds bet, as enjoyed by Pass Line players, the Don't Pass bettors laying Odds should hand their check to the dealer and announce that they're *laying Odds* on their Don't Pass bet. The dealer places the Odds checks tilted halfway over the check(s) in the straight Don't Pass bet. Assume the player is in a Double Odds casino and makes a $5 Don't bet and the point is 4. To lay full Odds, he must put up $20 to win $10 in addition to his $5 line bet. The $5 checks would be positioned by the dealer as shown in the diagram.

Like the line bet, the Odds bet may be retrieved at any time during a hand. Just tell the dealer, "Odds off." There is no percentage advantage or disadvantage either way for the player or the house on an Odds bet, so removing the bet only diminishes the action (and maybe profits).

THE PLAY

Full Odds are laid as follows for $10 Don't Pass bets in both a Single Odds or Double Odds casino. (These are the *maximum* amounts you can lay.)

$10 Don't Bet—Maximum Odds Lay

Point	Single Odds Lay	Double Odds Lay	To Win
4 or 10	$20	$40	1:2
5 or 9	$15	$30	2:3
6 or 8	$12	$24	5:6

By laying full Odds on the Don't Pass bets, the return on each dollar risked, including the line bet, is as follows:

Win Return Per Lay Dollar Risked

Point	Single Odds	Double Odds
4 or 10	.66	.60
5 or 9	.80	.75
6 or 8	.91	.88

While superficially it appears the better return is on Single Odds, the *profits* are less on a win, because the player has less money in action.

By laying Single Odds, the house advantage is reduced to 0.691 percent, and by laying Double

Odds, the house advantage diminishes to 0.459 percent (less than one half of 1 percent, which is the lowest vigorish on any bet in the entire casino).

COME BETS

A Come bet is exactly the same as a Pass bet. This bet is made in the space provided *after* the come-out roll and the shooter has a point. It's like starting over, creating a new point or a game within a game. The next roll becomes the come-out roll for the Come bet, and 7 or 11 wins; 2, 3, or 12 loses; 4, 5, 6, 8, 9, or 10 becomes the point for the Come bet.

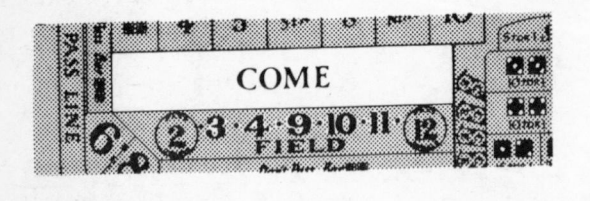

When a new point number is established for the Come bet, the dealer moves the Come bet to the corresponding numbered box on the layout to await a decision *for that point only*. Winning Come bets are paid off in the Come section where the bet was made as the dealer moves your bet out of the point number box. If the player does not then pick up the bet, the bet is in action the next roll for a come-out decision or another new point.

For very fast action, a Come bet may be made

on every roll of the dice. As with line bets, Odds can be *taken* with Come bets. Ask the dealer for the maximum amount of Odds on all Come bets.

For instance, say that the shooter already has a Pass Line point working. (The "buck" is in position on the line point number box.) The player makes a $10 bet in the Come section. If the next roll is a Crap (2, 3, or 12), the original line point is unaffected, but all Come bets lose. Should an "ee-yo 'leven" (11) be rolled, the line bet is unaffected, but the Come bet wins and pays off (1:1). Should a 7 be rolled, the line bets lose (seven-out), but the Come bet wins on the Natural. Should any of the five remaining point numbers be rolled, the Come bet will be moved to a certain position to identify the player in that point number's box and await a decision, Pass, or miss on each number.

Assume the player has a $10 Come bet on the 8 now waiting for the next roll. He can throw the dealer another $10 (Single Odds) and announce "Odds on the 8." The dealer will position the chips as shown.

The chips on top are the Odds bet. The player can take the Odds bet off anytime he wishes during a hand by telling the dealer "Odds off the 8," and the dealer will return the Odds bet.

Assume the shooter Passes on the original line point number as marked by the buck. Now the shooter will be coming out again; however, the player will still have his Come bet on the 8 working in the box. If the player also has Odds on his Come bet, he should announce to the dealer either "Odds off on the come-out" or "Odds working." In the case where the Odds are off, the dealer may not physically remove the Odds checks from the bet, but it's understood the bet is off. Then, in this case, if the shooter should throw a come-out 7, the original Come bet on the 8 would lose, but the Odds bet would be returned to the player, as it was understood to be "off."

The Come bet permits a player to participate in vigorous play by getting bets on all the box numbers (except the original line point) with the least amount of vigorish and then, in turn, take Odds on each number as it enters a box. This is done by placing a bet on Come before each roll. If the shooter has a "long hand," that is, he keeps throwing point numbers and no 7's, the player will find himself collecting with Odds on every roll. Such action is a possible way to make a big score in a hurry, provided the table is "hot" (Passing) and the hand is "long" (keeps rolling the numbers). Of course, when a 7 appears, the whole slate is wiped clean and all bets lose except the last Come bet, which wins. The action seems hectic to the outsider, but the play is really simple. The player in this instance is looking for lots of numbers and no 7's.

The house percentages on Come bets are the same as those for the Pass bets, an average of 98.59% return to the player and 1.41% profit to the house.

DON'T COME BETS

A Don't Come bet is the same as a Don't Pass bet. This bet is made after the come-out roll and the shooter has a point. Make this bet in the space provided and the next roll becomes the come-out roll for the Don't Come bet. In this case, 2 or 3 win (12 is a standoff); 7 or 11 lose; 4, 5, 6, 8, 9, or 10 becomes the point for the Don't Come bet.

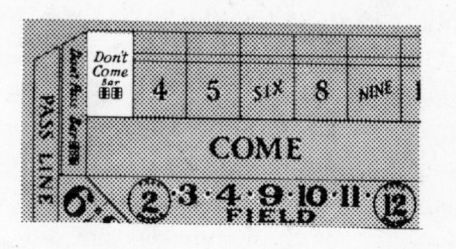

With a new point number, the dealer moves the Don't Come bet to the corresponding back numbered box on the layout to await a decision. Winning Don't Come bets are paid off where the bet was made. If not picked up immediately, the bet is in action the next roll.

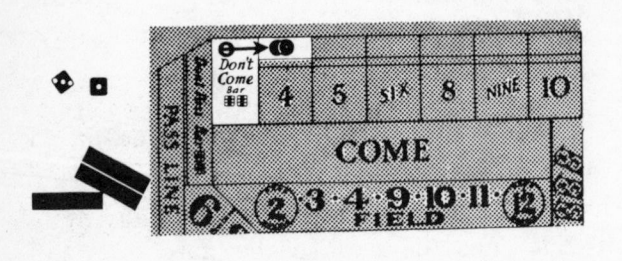

This action is the same fast action as the Come bet, only this time the player is betting against Passes and the long hand. For the fastest action, a Don't Come bet may be made every roll of the dice. Odds may be layed with all Don't Come bets. Again, ask the dealer for assistance.

The basic difference between Don't Come and Come bets is that the player can not only take the Odds off the box numbers at will, but he can retrieve the original Don't Come bet as well by notifying the dealer. Again, this is *not recommended*. The house percentages for this bet are the same as those given for Don't Pass and laying Odds.

PLACE BETS

At the rear of each half of the Craps table, stretching lengthwise, are six adjoining squares that are numbered 4, 5, 6, 8, 9, 10. These squares are used for holding Come bets and for indicating the Pass point by having a marker placed on the square whose number is that of the Pass point. These squares are also employed for holding Place bets, which are placed at the rear of the squares.

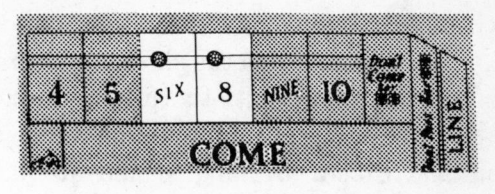

PLACE BETS ON 6 AND 8

A player can make a Place bet by placing a bet on any, some, or all the six indicated numbers. A bet placed on one of the numbers is a wager that that particular number will be rolled before a 7 is rolled. To make a Place bet, the player places his money on the table in front of a dealer and asks the dealer to place his bets on the particular numbers he wishes.

A Place bet is not a contract bet. It can be removed at any time. If a Place-bet bettor calls, "Down," he wants his Place bets picked up from the numbers and returned to him. If he calls, "Off," he wants his Place bets left on their numbers but out of play. After they have been called "Off," they are not wagers until he reinstates them by calling, "Working." Should a Place-bet number be rolled while the player's Place bets are "Off," he would not be paid any winnings; should a 7 be rolled while his Place bets are "Off," he would not suffer any losses. A bettor may qualify his "Off" call as "Off for the next roll" or "Off on the coming out," in which cases the Place bets would be back in action on the roll that followed the "Off" roll.

It is customary for the casino to handle all Place bets as being "Off" on the coming out of a new point. This happens when the shooter has just made a Pass by rolling his point at a time when there are Place bets on the numbers. It would be very inconvenient and time-consuming should all the Place bets be removed at this time only to be rebet after a new coming-out roll has established a new point. Also, should a new bettor have his Place bets removed at the completion of a winning point, he might not replace them, or probably not all of the amounts that were on them, after the dice have come out. The odds on these bets favor the casino much more than Pass and Come bets. Consequently, it is to the casino's advantage to have these bets reinstated, and so the casino by automatically taking them "Off" and then reinstating them, acts in a way that will encourage the player to keep his Place bets working.

Should the bettor wish to have his Place bets in effect on the coming-out roll, he will call, "Bets working on the come out," in which case a marker will be placed on one of his bets to show that they are all working.

Place bets pay premiums above the amounts bet. As a result, the minimum bet is $5 for Place bets on 4, 5, 9, and 10, and the minimum bet is $6 for Place bets on 6 and 8. Place bets in larger amounts are made up of multiples of these amounts.

If a 4 or a 10 Place bet becomes a winner, the winning amount is $9 for the $5 bet. The $9 is paid to the bettor, and his $5 Place bet remains working on the number unless he calls it "Down" or "Off." For a 5 or a 9 the payout is $7 for the $5 bet. The payout is also $7 for the $6 Place bets on 6 and 8.

Sometimes the Place bets are romanticized by saying that a Place bet is a combination of an even money bet and an Odds bet. The $5 Place bets on 4 and 10 are said to consist of a $1 even money bet and a $4 (quadruple) Odds bet, thus making the payout consist of $1 for the even money bet plus $8 for the odds (2:1) on the $4 bet. Likewise the $5 Place bets on 5 and 9 consist of a $1 even money bet and a $4 (quadruple) Odds bet, making a payout of $1 for the even money bet and $6 for the odds (3:2) on the $4 Odds bet. The 6 and 8 Place bets consist of a $1 even bet plus a $5 (quintuple) Odds bet, making a payout of $1 for the even money bet plus $6 for the odds (6:5) on the $5 Odds bet.

More simply put, the payouts are $9 for $5 bets on 4 and 10, $7 for $5 bets on 5 and 9, and $7 for $6 bets on 6 and 8.

Some casinos will permit smaller bets than $5.

They will permit bets of $3 on 4 and 10, with a payout of $5. They will also permit $3 bets on 5 and 9, with rewards of $4. On the Las Vegas Strip, $3 Place bets on 6 and 8 pay only $3 winnings. In downtown Las Vegas, where 50¢ chips are present, $3 Place bets on 6 and 8 pay winnings of $3.50, which gives them the same payout percent as the $7 that is paid for a $6 bet. In Atlantic City, casinos are never allowed to pay off at less than the approved payout odds on any bet. These odds are the same as usual in Nevada on Place bets—9:5 on 4 and 10, 7:5 on 5 and 9, 7:6 on 6 and 8.

The chart below shows the return ratios for the various Place bets in Las Vegas when payoffs vary according to the amount wagered.

Place Bet Number	Five-Dollar Return Ratio	Three-Dollar Return Ratio	
4	93.33%	88.88%	
5	96.00%	93.33%	
6	98.48%	90.91%	(Strip)
		98.48%	(Downtown)
8	98.48%	90.91%	(Strip)
		98.48%	(Downtown)
9	96.00%	93.33%	
10	93.33%	88.88%	
Place Bets as a group	96.27%	91.11%	(Strip)
		94.44%	(Downtown)

Besides the Place bets just mentioned, the Craps player also has the option of a "Place bet to lose," a Don't Place bet. This is a wager made at any time *against* any of the numbers 4, 5, 6, 8, 9 or 10. On this bet, the player wins when a 7 is thrown before the number bet against comes up. He loses if the number comes up before a 7 is rolled.

The payout odds are poor—in Atlantic City, 5:11 on 4 and 10, 5:8 on 5 and 9; and 4:5 on 6 and 8. In other words you would be risking $11 to win $5 on a Don't Place bet against the 4 or the 10. No experienced Craps player ever makes this bet. There are better ways to play your money. The payout odds may vary slightly in Nevada, but it's a bad bet there, too.

6 AND 8

At each end of the Craps layout, at its front corners, are two small adjoining squares. One is marked with a 6; the other is marked with an 8. A bet placed in either one of these boxes wagers that the number, either 6 or 8, whichever the bet is placed on, will be rolled before a 7 is rolled. These bets are not contract bets. They can be picked up at any time.

These bets pay no odds. They are even money bets, paying the same amount as the bet itself. Since there are six ways for rolling a 7 to five ways for rolling a 6 or an 8, the odds against winning either of these bets is 6:5 (six to five), which gives a

return ratio of 90.91% (10 units returned for each 11 units bet). This is the same ratio as that for a $3 Place bet on 6 or 8 in the $3 payoff casinos. The only differences between the two bets is that with the 6 and 8 bets the player places the bets himself and removes the winnings himself, whereas with Place bets the Dealer places the bets and removes them. Also the minimum bet of 6 and 8 can be less than $3, depending upon the house's minimum bet.

Because the odds on winning and losing are the same as for Place bets on the 6 or the 8, while the payout is usually less, if you are going to bet on either 6 or 8, make it a Place bet. Forget about betting the corner 6 or 8.

BUY BETS

Buy bets are the same as Place bets in that a Buy bet is another way to bet that a given point number *will be* rolled before a 7. The difference is in the way a Buy bet is made. The casino charges the player a straight 5 percent of the amount bet and pays winning bets at the correct odds (2:1, 3:2, or

6:5). As with Place bets, the bet can be made any time by handing the dealer the amount of the bet plus 5 percent commission. The minimum amount that can be wagered in this manner would depend on the table minimum—generally $5 on the 25¢ table, $20 on the $1 table. You give the dealer $21 to have a $20 bet. Since you automatically lose $1 for every $21 you put up, the house advantage is $1 \div 21 = 4.76\%$.

A Buy bet is identified in the box by a small button placed on top the stack by the dealer. This should not be confused as a 1:1 Come bet. A Buy bet is *not recommended*. A player who insists on betting the 5 or 9 should Place the bet; it has less vigorish.

LAY BETS

A Lay bet is the opposite of a Buy bet. It is a bet that a *7 will appear before a given point number*. The 5 percent commission is figured on the amount the player will *win*, not on the amount bet. The minimum amount that can be wagered in this manner would depend on the table minimum and the point. Ask the dealer about Lay bets. Lay bets are paid at correct odds. This is what the vigorish is on the various Lay bets:

- Lay bets on *4* or *10* pay 1:2 (2.44% vigorish)
- Lay bets on *5* or *9* pay 2:3 (3.22% vigorish)
- Lay bets on *6* or *8* pay 5:6 (4.00% vigorish)

HARD-WAY BETS

Rolling 4, 6, 8, 10 the "hard" way is a roll of doubles (2-2, 3-3, 4-4, 5-5). Hard-way bets may be made any time by throwing the bet to the Stickman, who will put it in the space provided on the

center portion of the layout. Players win Hard-way bets when the number is rolled the hard way *before a 7 and also before the same number total is rolled an easy way.* For example, a Hard-way bet on 4 wins if 2-2 is rolled before 1-3, 3-1, or any 7. The same principle is followed with 6, 8, or 10.

- Hard-way *4* or *10* pays 7 to 1 (88.88% return ratio)
- Hard-way *6* or *8* pays 9 to 1 (90.91% return ratio)

ONE-ROLL BETS

There are many bets offered on the Craps table that are decided by one roll of the dice. Sometimes a shooter will take a long time in deciding his Pass-point roll—maybe ten or fifteen rolls—and since this can be very boring for the neophyte Pass bettor, the casino table offers many delightful places for him to spend his money with fast-action, specifically one-roll bets.

Field Bets

On each half of the casino Craps table is a large blocked area in which are printed seven numbers—2, 3, 4, 9, 10, 11, 12. These are the Field numbers.

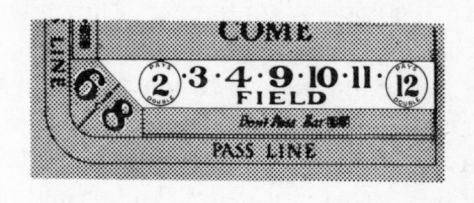

The temptation for making Field bets is very great for the uninitiated. The Field offers seven numbers, and if any of them appear on the next roll, the bettor wins. If any one of the other four numbers (5, 6, 7, 8) is rolled, he loses. Seven numbers to four numbers looks pretty good, especially to the novice bettor, but this Field is just another gimmick for enticing the player to place more money on the table with which to increase the casino's income.

The basic odds for the Field are very poor. There are just sixteen ways (one way to make a 2 plus two ways to make a 3 plus three ways to make a 4 plus four ways to make a 9 plus three ways to make a 10 plus two ways to make 11 plus one way to make 12) to make all the Field numbers out of thirty-six rolls. So the basic odds *against* rolling a Field number are 20:16, which gives a return ratio of 88.88%. Except generally for wagers on 2 and 12, Field bets are even money bets.

Because of the poor return ratio, some casinos, such as those on the Las Vegas Strip, give double payouts on 2's and 12's. This raises the Field return to eighteen and thus the return ratio to 94.44%.

Some casinos—including most of those in downtown Las Vegas—go further. They offer double returns on 2 and triple payouts on 12. This increases the Field payout to nineteen and raises the return ratio to 97.22%.

In Atlantic City, Field bets on 2 and 12 must always pay at least 2:1. (New Jersey law always allows casinos the option of paying off at higher odds if they choose to do so for competitive reasons.)

Other One-roll Bets

All one-roll bets other than the Field are placed in boxes that lie directly in front of the Stickman. Bets for these wagers are handed either to a dealer or to the Stickman, who places them in locations in their proper boxes so he can tell which bets belong to whom. Also directly in front of the Stickman are the boxes for the Hard-way bets. These bets are also handled only by the dealers and Stickman.

Bets on 7, 11, 2, 3, 12, or on Any Craps may be

made anytime. The bet is handed to the dealer or Stickman and is won or lost on the next roll of the dice.

- Bet on any *7* pays 4:1 (83.33% return ratio).
- Bet on Any Craps pays 7 to 1 (88.88% return ratio).
- Bet on either *3* or *11* in Nevada pays 14:1 or 15:1, depending upon casino policy (83.33% or 88.88% return ratio). In Atlantic City, the payoff is 15:1.
- Bet on either *2* or *12* in Nevada pays 29:1 or

30:1, depending upon casino policy (83.33%
or 86.11% return ratio). In Atlantic City,
the payoff is 30:1.

The C-E arrows surrounding the "prop box"
give the Stickman more betting spots for players
around the table to make the *Any Crap* or *11* bets,
as well as a combination of both. Any Crap bets are
placed on the "C" of an arrow pointing towards the
player. Likewise, a check will be placed on the "E"
for an 11 bet.

If the player bets double or more the table
minimum limit, he can call a *"Crap-eleven"* bet, and
the checks will be placed between the "C" and the
"E." However, half the player's bet actually goes
separately on each bet at the respective prevailing
odds on the layout. Of course, the player loses the
half that in effect has been bet on the losing proposition. These bets are *not recommended*.

A *Hop bet* (on the next "hop" of the dice) is
another one-roll bet that doesn't appear on the
layout. It is generally thrown to and held by the
Boxman, who simply remembers the player's bet.
Here the player asks for a specific combination of
the dice numbers. For instance, a "Hop Ace-Six" or
"Sixteen on the Hop" means that the player is
betting the next roll will show a 1-6 or 6-1. On all
Hop bets that are *not pairs*, the payoff is the same
as for an 11 on the layout. Hop bets that are pairs—
for example, "Hop thirty-three"—pay off the same

as for a "Deuce" on the layout. Again, these bets are *not recommended* because of the high vigorish.

The *Horn* bet may or may not have a designated space on the layout, but it can be called by the player. The minimum amount bet is four times the table minimum, as this is actually four bets covering the numbers 2, 3, 11, and 12 respectively. If any of these win, it is paid at the prevailing table odds for that number, but of course the player loses the three other, losing bets. This is a somewhat popular come-out bet in the Reno-Tahoe area.

The *Horn High* bet requires five minimum units and is essentially the same as the Horn bet, except one of the numbers is doubled. "Horn High eleven" means a single unit each on 2, 3, and 12, and two units on the 11. Again, Horn bets and Horn High bets are *not recommended*.

A seldom-called one-roll wager is the *Whirl* bet. It requires five minimum table units and covers all the *active* come-out numbers (2, 3, 7, 11, and 12). If hit, four bets will lose and the winning number will be paid at the odds given in the proposition box in the center of the layout. Should the 7 be rolled, the bet is a "push," a standoff—lose four and win four.

Players can make any of the proposition bets (Field, Hard-way, etc.) at the table. It is not required that they have a line bet on to qualify to make these bets. But players can then hold a spot at the table only by making Place bets, Field bets (not recommended), or Hard-way bets (not recommended either). The management does require that a reasonable amount of action be given, or a player will be asked to make room for more active players if conditions become crowded.

BET RETURN RATIOS

The following tabulation shows the bets and the return ratios of each offered by the casino Craps tables:

Bet	Return Ratio (%)
Don't Pass w/ D-Odds	99.54
Don't Come w/ D-Odds	99.54
Pass w/ D-Odds	99.394
Come w/ D-Odds	99.394
Don't Pass w/ S-Odds	99.31
Don't Come w/ S-Odds	99.31
Pass w/ S-Odds	99.15
Come w/ S-Odds	99.15
Don't Pass	98.59
Don't Come	98.59
Pass	98.59
Come	98.59
Place bet 6	98.48
Place bet 8	98.48
Field dbl. 2; trpl. 12	97.22
Place bets (group)	96.27

Place bet 5	96.00
Place bet 9	96.00
Field dbl. 2; dbl. 12	94.44
Place bet 4	93.33
Place bet 10	93.33
Six	90.91
Eight	90.91
Hard-way 6	90.91
Hard-way 8	90.91
Hard-way 4	88.88
Hard-way 10	88.88
Any Crap	88.88
Eleven (16 for 1)	88.88
Three (16 for 1)	88.88
Two (31 for 1)	86.11
Twelve (31 for 1)	86.11
Eleven (15 for 1)	83.33
Three (15 for 1)	83.33
Two (30 for 1)	83.33
Twelve (30 for 1)	83.33
Seven (5 for 1)	83.33
Under 7 (1 for 1)	83.33
Over 7 (1 for 1)	83.33

5

MONEY

MANAGEMENT

STRATEGY

It is difficult to tell or advise anyone how to handle his money in the casino. Craps games are hard to beat. The percentage works for the house on virtually every roll. The dice do go to extremes at times, and the only way to win large amounts is to take advantage of the extremes.

When you look at the return ratios of the bets offered at the Craps table, you may wonder how some people manage to lose so much money so quickly. With return ratios only as low as 83.33%, you may wonder why statistics show the take for the house to be between 20 and 30%. The reason for this is that people mismanage their betting. They do this either through their own stupidity or by following the suggestions of the Stickman, who concentrates on suggesting low return ratio bets.

ANY CRAP "INSURANCE"

Many players believe that it is sophisticated betting to "insure" their Pass bets by protecting them with an Any Crap bet on their coming-out roll. Since the Any Crap bet returns eight for one (seven unit wins), a $7 Pass bet would require a $1 bet on Any Crap for this insurance. Then, should a Crap appear on the coming-out roll, the player would lose his $7 Pass bet, but in its place he would receive a $7 profit from his Any Crap bet. He would suffer no loss. This is the explanation for justifying the use of the Any Crap bet as insurance, but what kind of money management is it when a $7 bet with a 98.59% return ratio is protected by a $1 88.88% return ratio bet? The player would be better off in the long run, since he has shown his willingness to speculate a total of $8 on the roll, to bet the entire $8 at the 98.59% return ratio on the Pass Line.

The Stickman is an expert at selling this "insurance" bet and also all the other low-return bets. When the dice are coming out he will ask, "Anyone for insurance?" or if someone has already placed an Any Crap bet, "Anyone else for insurance?" He usually means to imply, "Some intelligent bettor has done this, why don't you?"

This act of talking suckers into putting money on Any Crap bets on the coming-out roll is just the beginning of the Stickman's skullduggery. Suppose a Crap does come up on the roll. No one has really won anything, nor has the house lost anything, but the stage has been set for the great fleece.

This is how that comes about: Neither the dealers nor the Stickman remove the original bets from the Any Crap box. They pay the profits to the players. A Stickman can make quite a show with these payoffs. Suppose a player had "insured" a $100 Pass bet with a $15 Any Crap bet and then a Crap was thrown. The Stickman will leave the $15 in the Any Crap box, tap his stick in front of the player, and tell the dealer, "Pay the man $105." By bringing attention to this payoff, the Stickman makes it sound as though the player has won $105, whereas he is actually only $5 ahead. Meanwhile the $15 is still at risk. Such antics by the Stickman encourage other bettors who have perhaps lost their Pass bets by not having had them insured to "protect" themselves on this next coming-out roll.

This player who has just "insured" himself again (by leaving the $15 in place) on this new coming-out roll after a Crap is no longer buying his insurance at the 88.88% return ratio rate he faced the first time. He is buying it at an *18.5% return ratio* rate. That is right, an 18.5% return ratio! The Stickman has done his job, because low return ratios like this are what the casinos wish the players faced on every bet.

MONEY STRATEGY

When players place their bets on Any Crap on the next roll following the roll of a Crap, they are actually betting that two Craps will be rolled in succession. It makes no difference whether the bet has been made before the first Crap has been rolled or after a Crap has been rolled. It is still a bet that two Craps will be rolled in succession.

If one unit were bet that two Craps would be rolled in succession, so that after the first Crap the eight-unit return would be parlayed and bet on the rolling of a second Crap, the return ratio would be 79% (8 units × 8 = 64 units return, with a probability of 9 × 9; 64/81 × 100 = 79%). However, in the case where a payoff of seven units has been made after the first Crap, leaving only one unit to be bet at 8:1 on the second Crap, the final return for the two bets would be fifteen (7 + 8); the return ratio would be 15/81 × 100 = 18.5%. In the case where the players did not bet on the first Any Crap and only on the second, the return ratio is even lower (9.88%) because the return in this case is only eight units with the same probablility of 81:1 against a Crap being rolled (8/81 × 100 = 9.88%).

OTHER PROPOSITION BETS

The same mathematical principle applies to all the bets under the control of the Stickman, including the Hard-ways, whose profits he joyfully calls out to be paid to the lucky bettors by the dealers while leaving the original unit bet sitting happily (for the house) at a very low return ratio. It is because of the low return ratios that Hard-way bets are not automatically taken off with the coming-out roll of a new Pass Line decision. The low return ratios are too favorable for the house.

A simple rule to follow, without exception, is *never to place bets on any of the low-return ratio proposition bets that fill the box spaces in front of the Stickman.*

All other table bets, except for 6 and 8 (at the corners), give higher return ratios than those controlled by the Stickman. However, these should still be examined closely and not accepted blindly on the basis of the order of their general return ratios, because the circumstances surrounding the bet can alter actual return ratios greatly.

ODDS BETS

On the surface, Odds bets, because of the high return ratios their applications yield, appear to be the proper bet to make at every opportunity. *Don't accept this.*

When there are no Odds, there will theoretically, out of 1980 Pass Line decisions, be 1004 losses to 976 wins for a house profit of 28 (1004 − 976) betting units. The profit to the house will be 1980 unit bets × 1.41% = 28 units.

When there are Single Odds, there will theoretically be 3300 unit bets; 1980 + (1980 × $2/3$) × .0085 = 28 unit profit.

When there are Double Odds, there will be 4620 unit bets; 1980 + (1980 × ⅔) + (1980 × ⅔) × .00606 = 28 units profit.

This means simply that if the dice perform according to their theoretical normal odds there will be a 28-unit profit from 1980 Pass Line decisions regardless of whether Single Odds, Double Odds, Triple Odds or whatever are applied to those decisions that are not decided by one roll. Odds are a standoff bet. They produce neither winnings nor losses when the dice's performance is theoretically normal. Because of the large increases in the number of units bet when Odds are applied, should the dice perform at a return ratio lower than 98.59% and Single Odds be applied, they will produce losses 1⅔ times greater than had no Odds been applied. At Double Odds, the loss would be 2⅓ times greater.

Should the dice perform at a return ratio greater than 98.59%, the winnings would be greater (or the losses would be less, depending upon the magnitude of the return ratio increase).

Odds should be bet only when the dice are performing in a winning manner. Until a *new player* has developed a feel for when this might happen, he *should not experiment with Odds*.

The same conclusion for Odds as applied to the Pass Bets applies to the Come Bets.

PASS AND COME BETS

When either a Pass point is established or when a Come-bet point is set, the odds against this point's being made change from the 1004 to 976 with its 98.59% return ratio to much lower return ratios. The 4 and 10 have odds of 2:1 *against* them, giving them a 67% return ratio. The 5 and 9 have an 80% return ratio, and the 6 and 8 a 90.91% return ratio.

The Pass bet and the Come bet are contract bets. They must remain in effect until a decision is reached. Naturally the house is pleased to have bets with such low return ratios gracing its tables.

Odds will raise the return ratios of these bets— the 4 and 10 to 83.33%, the 5 and 9 to 90%, and the 6 and 8 to 95.44%. The Odds bets are not contract bets and can be removed at any time. As a matter of practice, the house automatically considers all Odds bets on Come numbers to be "off" on the coming-out roll of a Pass Line decision, so after a Pass point has been made, the Come bets are still working and the Odds are off. The house wants only the best for itself—low return ratios. In order to keep the Come-bet Odds in effect, the player must instruct the dealer that his Odds are "working."

Come bets have the same return ratios as the Pass bet, but this does not mean that playing the Come bets at every opportunity will result in a theoretical loss equal to that of the Pass bet.

The average number of dice rolls encountered in a Pass Line decision is 3.36. Consequently, should a Pass bet of one unit and a Come bet of one unit be made at every opportunity, the theoretical loss for the Pass and Come bets combined would be $28 \times 3.36 = 94$ units, which means that the Come bets, with a return ratio the same as that of the Pass bet, will lose 66 units, compared to 28 units lost by the Pass bet.

It might seem that Come bets prosper whenever Pass bets prosper, but this is not necessarily true. Pass bets produce their largest winnings during a "hot hand." Come bets have their best performances during "long hands." A hand has to be both "hot" and "long" for both to prosper.

A "hot hand" is a shooter's hand that has a large number of Passes. These Passes can contain 7's and 11's, which they usually do, as well as Pass points. The 7's work to the detriment of Come bets. A "long hand" is a shooter's hand that has a large number of rolls without any 7's. Because a 7 will erase all Come bets, a long hand is necessary in order to earn appreciable winnings from Come bets.

Until a player has developed a feel for when a long hand might occur, he should not experiment with the Come bet.

PLACE BETS

Place bets offer interesting opportunities. Some people will cover all the Place bets. This requires a 32-unit placement. In order just to break even, it requires a minimum of four winning rolls. Some people will place bets on just the 6 and 8. Some will select other numbers. All these people are betting blindly, hoping for a long hand.

Come bets benefit from a long hand. Supposing instead of Come bets we used the Come-bet format for making Place bets. If a 4 is rolled, instead of making a Come bet of 4 with a return of 10 units (5 + 5) if another 4 is then rolled, we could make a Place bet on 4 with a return of 14 units (5 + 9). What we would actually be doing would be switching from a bet with a 67% return ratio to one with a 93.33% return ratio, and this switch to a higher return ratio holds for all the other numbers in this situation.

Even if Double Odds are placed on the Come bets, the returns will be greater for the Place bets. If we assume a 10-unit Come bet followed by a 20-unit Double Odds bet and compare the results to Place bets of 30 units (the same amount as 10 + 20 on the Come bets), we find that for completed bets the Come bets on 4 and 10 would return 80 units while the Place bets would return 84. For 5 and 9, the Come bets would return 70 units, and the Place bets would return 72. For 6 and 10, the Come bets would return 64 units and the Place bets 65.

When a 7 is rolled during a Pass point decision, play stops for both the Come bets and for the Place bets. This 7 makes a win for the last Come bet and does nothing for the Place bet. Elevens will produce wins for the Come bets and nothing for the Place bets. Craps will make losses for the Come bets and do nothing for the Place bets. But, regardless of these differences, mathematically, Place bets will always give higher returns than Come bets.

Place Bets have another great advantage— they can be removed in their entirety at any time. Only the Odds can be removed from the Come bets.

When the coming-out roll is made, after a Pass point has been won, only the Odds can be "Off" on the Come bets, whereas the entire bet is "Off" with the Place Bets. And should a 7 be rolled, the Come bets still remaining would become losses. There would be no losses for the Place bets.

When a player has graduated from the minimum house bet to the $5 chip, then is the time for him to begin to consider the Place bets, not before. He should forget about Come bets at the very beginning of his Craps-shooting experiences. And as mentioned previously, he should forget about Don't Place bets altogether.

FIELD BETS

The Field bet with double 2 and triple 12 might look like a fair risk at a 97.22% return ratio. However, when we recognize that a Field bet can be made every time the dice are rolled, which means 1980×3.36, and that the percent loss would be 2.78%, we can see that the loss on the 1980 theoretical rolls would be $1980 \times 3.36 \times .0278 = 185$ units. If you were on the Las Vegas Strip, where only double 2 and double 12 are paid, the loss would be

359 betting units. Need we say anything more than that *the Field is not a profitable way to spend the day.*

DON'T PASS AND DON'T COME BETS

When either a Don't Pass point or a Don't Come point is established, the odds against the Don't Pass and Don't Come points winning change from 976:949 with a 98.59% return ratio to much higher return ratios. The 4 and 10 have odds of 2:1 favoring them, giving them a return ratio of 133.34%. The 5 and 9 have odds of 3:2 favoring them, giving them a return ratio of 120%, and the 6 and 8 have odds of 6:5 favoring them, giving them a return ratio of 109%.

Laying Odds on these bets would lower the return ratios but in no case to below 100%, because the Odds are a 1:1 bet. Laying Odds on Don't Pass points and Don't Come points can be extremely expensive. It is best to leave these betting experiences to someone else.

Don't Pass points and Don't Come points are not contract bets. They can be removed at any time. Naturally the casino sees it this way and hopes that the bettor will remove them, because these points very greatly favor the bettor.

Don't Pass Points and Don't Come points should *never* be removed.

The Bias Against Don't Bets

We have been studying primarily the Pass side of the game and have built cases endorsing only two bets on this side—the Pass bet and the Place bet. The Don't side represents the other half of this game. Even though almost half of the decisions on the coming-out roll are Don't Pass (949 Don't to 976 Pass), relatively few players engage in Don't bets. The reason is very simple: Don't bets are not exciting.

When a "hot" hand or a long hand appears, it is rolled by just one person, and the table may have chips resting on the side bets during many Passes until the shooter sevens-out. The action is fast, and the players around the table get more excited as their bets multiply. When a series of consecutive Don't Pass bets occur—and there are about as many of these as there are series of consecutive Passes—each Don't Pass win will probably be made by a different shooter. The chips do not build up on the side bets, because the table is emptied after each Don't Pass win. The play is slow and dull and Pass-oriented players will leave the table.

FORMULA FOR PLAY

A new player should restrict himself to the Pass bet, using the house minimum bet. Once he has gained a feel for the dice and if he has doubts about the dice continuing in a Pass-winning way, he should experiment with not betting, that is, study the action more to familiarize himself with play, making mental bets as practice. If he finds himself fairly successful, he can then replace his not-betting cycle with Don't Pass bets.

One danger will appear at this time: the temptation to try to guess the direction of every Pass Line decision. There is no way to predict the next Pass Line decision with any accuracy. Only long trends can be surmised. During many long down trends, a "hot" hand will appear where a shooter will make five, six, or more passes. These do not necessarily signal a change in dice direction. More likely, the dice are taking a short recess from their continuing slide.

As a player gets more comfortable and more successful first with his Pass and then his Don't Pass betting, he can increase the amount he bets, and when he reaches the $5 chip he can begin his experiments with the Place bets.

During this educational period, the player should observe the antics of the Stickman and see what happens to the bankrolls of players who follow the Stickman's advice. When either a "hot" hand or a long hand appears, he should study how well the players take advantage of it.

After particularly active long hands during which the players have been screaming and cheering, this new player should study where the chips that are left had been bet. He will find the Hardways and the Come bets loaded. Most of the cheering will have been because bettors were seeing their wagers parlay on Come bets with Odds, not because they were pocketing profits. The smart players will have utilized Place bets and have taken their profits and most of their bets "down" before the final crash.

THINGS TO REMEMBER

1. You figure to lose every time you play.
2. Play the minimum size chip until thoroughly familiar with Craps.
3. When you are a winner and the dealers have been helpful, thank them by occasionally making a bet for them on 11. Toss your chip in front of the Stickman and say, "Eleven for the boys." If it's a dollar and an 11 shows on the next roll, you're a nice person who just "toked" $15.
4. Don't drink too much, as booze will help you lose.
5. Don't play when overly tired.
6. Never try to recoup losses by increasing your unit bet. The only time to increase your betting unit is when you are winning.
7. People with no plan—people who just come to play—will never stop until either the time or money runs out. Most often it's the money.
8. Play for recreation only. Have lots of fun and don't get hurt.
9. This book is a book on how to begin playing Casino Bank Craps in a sensible, safe way. Before joining the boys in the "hot" hand and long hand events, study further. There are books that discuss in much more detail what can be expected from these events.

6

CRAPS

TABLE ETIQUETTE

There are many rules concerning the handling of the dice at Craps tables. These are designed primarily as safeguards against the possibilities of having crooked dice substituted at the table.

1. *A player handles the dice only when he is shooting them.* He never picks them up and hands or rolls them back to the shooter, even though the Stickman might mistakenly have placed them in front of him.

2. If one of the dice flies off the table during a roll, which happens occasionally, *a player may pick up the die from the floor, but he should not throw it back on the table.* Instead, *he should hand it to one of the dealers*, who in turn will hand it to the Boxman, who will examine it before returning it to

the Stickman. If a die from another table lands near you, pick it up and hand it to one of the players at the other table. He can then hand it to one of his dealers. *Never throw a die onto a table.* It could land while a roll is in progress.

3. *Never rest your elbows on the rail of the table in such a manner that any part of your hands or arms extends over the table.* These protruding hands or arms could interfere with a roll of the dice and, if hit by the dice, effect a losing roll. Any willful action that interferes with the free throw of the dice is frowned upon, and a continuation of such action could result in the player's being asked to leave the table.

Occasionally, a person's hand will be hit by the dice when he is in the process of making a bet. Sometimes this is due to the player having been slow in placing his bet; sometimes it is due to the Stickman's not having noticed that the player was in the process of making a bet when he released the dice to the shooter. Regardless whose fault it is, the Stickman will remind the player to make his bets *before* the dice are thrown. It is the player's responsibility to see that the dice are not in action whenever he places his bets.

4. In front of the Stickman is a dish in which there are usually five or more dice. When the dice have passed to a new shooter, the Stickman empties the dice in the dish onto the table and then with his stick pushes them before the new shooter. He will

hold them there until all coming-out bets have been made before releasing his stick so the new shooter can select two dice for his roll. The Stickman then slides the other dice back to the dish and places them into it. *The only time the Stickman touches the dice with his fingers is when he lifts them, in full view of all players, from the table in front of his dish into the dish.* He never transports them across the table in his hands.

After each roll by a shooter, the Stickman recovers the dice with his stick and holds them on the table in full view of all the players until the dealers have paid all bets and new bets have been made. He then slides them with his stick to the shooter. This process is repeated with the same dice until the shooter has sevened out. At this time the Stickman slides the dice in front of his dish and places them in it with the other dice so that he can offer all the dice to the new shooter.

5. *After the new shooter has selected his dice, he must roll them toward the end of the table that is farthest from him.* Since the Stickman stands at the middle of the table, the dice must always be thrown past him. When the dice change ends, the Stickman will always announce, "Dice coming out new direction."

6. It is a rule at Craps tables that the shooter *bounce the dice off the back of the table farthest from him.* If a shooter occasionally has one die not

get that far, his rolls will be considered legitimate, but if a player consistently fails to get the dice to the back of the table despite warnings by the Stickman, he may have his rolling privilege revoked and be asked to pass the dice.

If a die lands on top of or winds up leaning against a chip on the table that has been bet by a player, it is a legal roll. However, should a die land in the Stickman's dish or come to rest on top of any of the chips stacked in front of the dealers, even though it is sitting upright and not cocked, the roll is void and the decision must be determined by the next roll.

7. After a shooter has selected his dice, he may do many things. He may make them rattle by shaking them. He may make several short rolls in front of him pretending to fend off bad luck. He may pick them up and throw them quickly. But *the shooter must keep the dice always in full view of all the players and the house men.* If he picks up the dice and lowers his hand out of sight behind the table even for an instant, his roll is disallowed and he will be asked to surrender the dice to the Boxman for examination. The shooter then selects new dice, even though the ones he surrendered have been placed back into the Stickman's dish (assuming the Boxman judges them legitimate).

8. *The shooter may ask for new dice at any time.* He is not bound to continue rolling the ones he

first selected. When the shooter asks for new dice, the Stickman will empty his dish and push the dice to the shooter so he can make another selection.

9. When a shooter has a die fly off the table, it is his privilege to demand that the die be recovered so he can continue playing with the same dice. When a die flies off the table, the shooter must call, "Same dice" quickly so the Stickman can hear him. Otherwise the Stickman will place the die remaining on the table in the dish, upset the dish, and push all the dice to the shooter. It is the Stickman's job to keep the game moving quickly.

7

GETTING THE MOST

OUT OF

CASINO PLAY

In reading these pages you will have gained a better insight into the game and enough basic knowledge to add to your enjoyment of it. Keep in mind that the casino has the advantage in every game. The odds are always against you. So play for fun rather than out of a determination to win. But take it seriously enough to get the most value out of your gambling dollar.

Many players don't take casino games seriously enough to bother learning anything about them in detail. Those are the players the casino loves. They take long shots, generally play unwisely, and usually lose quickly. A knowledgeable player aware of game details will play more intelligently and enjoy a longer game with more excitement. That player also stands a better chance of winning.

Here are sound guidelines to follow for getting the most out of casino play:

- *Learn as much as you can about the games you play.* Familiarize yourself with the rules and the play options before you commit your money. Don't jump into the game blind. Gambling is a business with the casino, not a game. When it comes to getting value for your money, you will do best if you approach each play situation from a businesslike perspective, paying full attention to details.

- *Stay sober.* Sobriety is a priority if you are to make sound judgments on committing your money in play. The casino dealers aren't drinking alcohol; you're better off avoiding it, too. Stick to juice, soda, or coffee. Stick to the business at hand so you make businesslike play decisions. That's not to say you can't have fun. In fact, you will find that serious, sober play proves more challenging and enjoyable over the long run.

- *Keep yourself fresh.* Avoid stress. Take frequent rest breaks. Never play when you're tired, as that affects your judgment.

Most players who overextend themselves financially do so simply because they fail to pace themselves. You are better off playing short sessions than trying to make a big score in one long session. Don't keep pushing yourself. Even if you're winning and feel "hot," don't get caught up to the extent that you risk your profits.

If you feel tired or irritable, it's time to relax. Get away from the casino awhile and regain your composure. Evaluate your financial situation, your emotions and mental stamina, your physical condition. More importantly, reevaluate your playing session. How did you play? Were you making intelligent decisions? Did you find yourself forsaking knowledge to play hunches? Be honest with yourself. What do you think you did right/wrong? The answers to these questions will reveal much about you as a player. Stay alert. Only you can tell if you were defeating yourself by your manner of play.

● **_Remember that you are playing with real money._** While we use the terms _play_ and _game_, this is not child's play. The casino takes it seriously enough to make you use real money instead of allowing you to wager with marbles or jellybeans. Take your play as seriously as any other activity that requires you to lay your money on the line.

Chips and tokens are money. Don't be fooled by the play money effect. The casino tries to soften the reality of risking hard cash by giving you plastic chips and tokens to play with, but they do have monetary value. There's a very evident psychological effect to the use of chips. Let's face it, a stack of them being swept away after a losing outcome doesn't hurt as badly as seeing a stack of hard-earned dollars being swept away.

Chips and tokens are also advantageous to the casino because people are more inclined to play them all than to go to the trouble of cashing them in. Often players feel they must play them rather than cash them in. But you pay for them, and they do have a cash-in value. Don't let the casino fool you and don't fool yourself into thinking chips and tokens are just something to play with. They are money!

• *Don't blame other people for your losses.* Nobody makes you lose. The dealer has no control over you, nor do the other players. The decision on what and how to bet is yours alone. You're the one who makes the choices.

Sometimes even a winner will have a nasty attitude. He thinks he should have played more to win more or blames another player for keeping him from winning more than he did. This is unwarranted and unnecessary. The mature player recognizes responsibility for his own play decisions, win or lose. If you don't get the result you want from your bet, don't assume a childlike attitude of "getting even." Besides, who will you get even with? The dealer? The other players? The casino? There's no one to get even with.

Nobody is forcing you to gamble. You know the odds are against you. You know the possibility of losing is very real, so accept it when it happens. Be prepared to lose!

• *Don't trust to luck.* There is no such thing as luck; you either win or lose. The outcome of the play decision is the bottom line. It is either favorable or unfavorable. Luck is a myth. The mathematics and the odds are immutable in each game, the same for players feeling "lucky" as for players feeling "unlucky." Making bets according to how lucky you feel rather than on a realistic calculation of odds only puts you more at the mercy of the odds, and these are always against you.

● *Don't count on "hot" or "cold" roulette wheels, cards, dice, etc.* While there will be cycles of events, the random process games are just that, random. The instruments of play have no memory; they are not self-controlled and are not responsible in any way for their actions or results. A "hot" or "cold" session exists only in one's mind. A "hot" session for one player is a "cold" session for another. It all boils down to who won or lost. The wagering decision was either right or wrong. That's the bottom line every time.

● *Beware of overconfidence.* When we win we feel good. When we win big we may feel as if we own the world, that we're something special. We're suddenly on a roll, and now is the time to play hard for all the times we lost.

This is when we are most inclined to have a drink or two, to get loose and "live it up." We become careless, reckless, and irresponsible. With our defenses down, we proceed to ignore little things like odds, percentages, and reasonable bet limits. Like a big, powerful ship going full speed without a rudder, we play on and on, following no particular set course. And where do we end up? In the casino's dry dock, that's where.

When you win, whether big or small, keep from developing an overconfident attitude. Keep your wits about you at all times. Don't throw caution to the winds. If you won, see it as the result of a successful business decision, not as an indication that things are now going your way. The outcome of your bet was favorable, that's all. The next bet is its own event and isn't influenced by the events of the previous roll or hand. Keep your feet on the ground and you'll more likely keep at least some of your winnings in your pocket.

• *Don't count on some system to strike it rich.* Systems can sometimes help you develop a play strategy and thereby add to the interest of the game. They are not necessarily reliable investment guides. Committing money according to a system, particularly one advocating increasing wagers upon a loss because then a win is "due," is often just another way to lose money. Systems players in many cases do no better than systematically lose. (However, this does not include card counting strategies for blackjack, as these are not considered systems but proven techniques when properly applied.)

• *Ask questions whenever there is something you don't understand.* Dealers will be happy to explain anything you don't understand. Again, most applicable information is available in books. You can save yourself a lot of uncertainty—and money—by reading up on a game before undertaking play. If you decide to learn by experience, it will cost you many times more than a couple of books. The advantage of a book is that you can go through it at your own pace. By learning what's recommended and what to avoid *before* you go to the casino, you'll save yourself a lot of grief.

Casino play will teach you in time, but those lessons can get awfully expensive. And once at the casino, don't be intimidated into playing along without understanding what's happening. Ask questions when in doubt about anything. Don't risk proving a sucker for fear of appearing uninformed.

● *Always practice good money management.* That is critical. If you can't manage your money, you shouldn't gamble. Don't get extravagant or erratic in your betting. Play at a level you can comfortably afford. Don't try to impress other people. Playing to put on a show for other people can prove awfully expensive, and chances are they're much less interested in your performance than in their own. Handle bets as business decisions and concentrate on informed strategy when making them.

● *Be sensible about "toking."* If you feel generous, you may tip the dealers. Or if you win at slots, tip the change girl; if you win at Keno, tip the writers.

But don't tip at random! If you win at blackjack, craps, roulette, or baccarat, tip at the end of your playing session. This is fair to you and to the dealers. While you could toke after every win, you will find that doing so cuts down on your playing capital. It isn't unusual to see a player consistently tip throughout a session only to discover afterward that he or she has given the dealers much more than was won.

Suppose you play and win thirty times during a session. If you toke the dealer each time, he will certainly be most gracious, but you are defeating yourself in the long run. At the end of the session, which will inevitably include losses, you may come out only a few dollars ahead or even be down a few dollars. Meanwhile you have literally given some of your capital away to the dealer. By waiting until the end of the session, you can more accurately evaluate your win/loss situation and toke accordingly, if at all.

Toke only if you feel it is warranted. Dealers generally work for minimum wage or just a little more than that. They depend on tokes to supplement their low wages, and they work hard for their money. So if they have treated you courteously, toke them as you would a waiter or waitress for good service. But if they are "toke hustling" or obviously hinting for a toke, do *not* tip them. They should not be allowed to do this. In many casinos, employees caught toke hustling will be fired.

If you win big, however—several hundred or several thousand dollars—don't insult the dealer by throwing him a nickel chip ($5). That would be like giving a waiter in a restaurant a penny. Show honest appreciation. There is nothing more denigrating than having a gambler win several thousand dollars and then give the dealer a $5 or $10 toke.

The decision to toke is, of course, yours and yours alone. There is no rule stating that it is mandatory to toke anybody for anything. It is strictly a convention of courtesy, a way to say "thanks." After all, it is your money, and they don't toke you when the house wins.

● *Don't boast about your winnings.* Announcing your winnings can be an open invitation to trouble from muggers and thieves. Similarly, don't flash your money. Be careful at all times. Don't carry large amounts of chips or cash around the casino with you. It's better to keep large amounts with the casino's cashier. You can withdraw what you want as you "need" it, and you won't have to worry about potential trouble from strangers. It's an unpleasant fact that casinos at times attract people who aren't there to play the games offered but to take advantage of unwary, careless players. When it comes to money, the old watchword "out of sight, out of mind" is the key to avoiding trouble.

There are many more points of practice that could be covered in detail, but these are the most important considerations. As a rule, you will find that survival in the casino is a matter of using common sense. Don't let the exotic setting, the excitement of play, or the prospects of a possible big money win cloud your judgment. You'll have more fun if you take a sensible approach to the entertainment opportunities offered in the casino.

APPENDIX—

DEALERS' INSTRUCTIONS

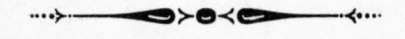

What follows is a copy of the mimeographed instructions given to newly employed Craps dealers in one downtown Las Vegas casino.

DEALERS

1. *Repeat all bets.*
2. *Change and payoffs are to be made on Come Line in front of you.*
3. *Let Stickman mention all proposition bets to players.*
4. *When paying a Place bet or Buy bet, there is no need to ask player, "Same bet?" or "Do you wish to press it?" Give him the money, and let him make the decision.*
5. *Since the Stickman made the announcement on bets being off coming out, there is no need to*

stop a game and ask a player. Exception: *A player whose bets are sometimes off and sometimes work should be asked.*

6. *Keep cigarettes and other things out of your shirt pockets while on table.*

7. *Show Boxman both sides of hands when being relieved. No need to clap them.*

8. *Help the Stickman by watching the dice when shooter has dice on your end. Protect yourself and your fellow dealers.*

9. *Pay only one bet at a time. This way, you can be sure a bet is right, and you won't have to return.*

10. *Watch your end.*

11. *Don't lay on one hand and deal with the other. This is a bad habit, and hard to break once you get it.*

12. *If a Boxman or Pit man tells you to hold a bet, stop. We all make mistakes!*

13. *Don't cap bets.*

14. *If a player requests a drink, tell the Boxman.*

15. *If a player tosses a bill on the layout, call "Change Only," unless he calls for a certain bet.*

16. *If you do not understand a bet and the dice are rolling, tell the player, "No action this roll." Do it in a nice way.*

17. *Put change for a bill in front of the player who gives it to you. Call all change.*

18. *Put payoff in front of player it belongs to.*

19. *Do not put payoffs or change in player's hands.*
20. *"Buddy," "Pal," and "this woman" are not good terms to use to players. "Sir" and "Lady" or "Miss" are appreciated much more.*
21. *Wear your I.D. badge at all times.*
22. *Never, for any reason, toss or throw chips or money at player.*

STICKMEN

1. *Keep your eyes on dice, while in shooter's hand, at all times. After dice leave shooter's hand, keep eyes on shooter's hand for a split second to make sure the hand is clean.*
2. *Stickmen always have the right-of-way; so after dice settle and call is made, bring dice to the outside of the Pass Line, then to the center of the table.*
3. *Watch all payoffs on your end. When payoffs are complete, check other end before letting dice go.*
4. *Watch your end (the way the dice are traveling).* Exception: *Boxman asks you to watch other end.*
5. *Be courteous to all players.* This is important!
6. *Craps, 7, and 11 will be mentioned on every come-out roll—not just one of these.*
7. *Repeat all proposition bets* loud and clear.
8. *When paying a proposition bet, announce:* "And you're still up the same way."
9. *Announce: All Odds, Place bets, and Buy bets*

are *automatically off, and Hard-ways work unless otherwise specified.*

10. *Do not talk across the table when a game is in progress.*

11. *Call all mistakes you see.* This *is what makes a top Stickman.*

12. *Keep control of game at all times.*

13. *Do not argue on table—if you ask a player to please hit the end, or try to speed up a slow player, etc., ask them only once, then let the Boxman take over.*

14. *If you don't understand a bet or don't hear it and the dice are in the air, call, "No bet this roll."*

15. *Get as many rolls as you can—time is of the essence.*

16. *Place all proposition bets correctly. If you are not sure, ask the dealer whose bet it is.*

17. *When you have watched the payoffs on your end, check center for bets to be sure layout is clear of losing bets.*

18. *Get yours first—then pay.*

19. *Do not make change from stick.*

20. *A short pause after the come-out roll will give the players a chance to make their bets.*

21. *A good Stickman calls the numbers* loud and clear.

GLOSSARY

ace — the 1-spot on a die.

action — the play or betting. Heavy betting is big or fast action.

Back Line — same as Don't Pass Line.

Bank Craps — type of Craps played in casinos; where players wager against the house or banker.

bar — not allowed. Barring 12 or 2 on Don't Pass bets enables the casino to accept Don't bets.

bet — wager made by the player in a casino.

bet the limit — to wager the maximum allowed by the casino.

Big 6 or 8 — a bet made on either 6 or 8 that it will be rolled before 7 (pays 1 to 1).

boards — the raised portion around the table. Back-board, rail.

Boxman — the casino employee who supervises the Craps game and deposits currency in the drop-box.

box numbers — the six point numbers (4, 5, 6, 8, 9, 10). Numbered boxes in which Come, Place and Buy bets are put until a decision. Also Place numbers, Off numbers.

buck — a marker used to indicate the point number and if Odds are on or off on the come-out roll.

Buy bets — a bet made on a point number that the number will be rolled before a 7 is rolled. 5% charge.

Call bet — a verbal wager made by known players.

casino — a place where games of chance are conducted.

casino manager — the general manager of the casino.

check — the markers used in place of currency. A chip, non-metallic.

chip — token or marker used in place of currency. In the casino they are called checks.

chop — term to designate dice action of win-lose, win-lose, win-lose, etc.

Come bet — same as a Pass bet, but made when the shooter has a point. A "new" point.

come-out roll — the first roll after a Pass Line decision.

"Coming out" — the Stickman's call to alert the players to make the bets on Pass Line and Don't Pass Line.

commission — the 5% charged Buy bets.

Craps — a gambling game using dice. The name of the numbers 2, 3, or 12 in this game.

credit manager — casino employee who decides whether to accept the player's personal check.

croupier — a French term for the dealer.

dealer — croupier. Person conducting the game.

deuce — the 2-spot on a dice.

dice — plural of die. By usage in the casino, acceptable when referring to one die or a pair.

die — small cube marked from 1 through 6.

Do bettor — Pass Line bettor.

Don't bettor — Don't Pass Line bettor.

Don't Come — same as Don't Pass bet, but made after the shooter has a point.

Don't Pass — a bet that the shooter loses.

drop box — a box fastened to the under side of the table, where all cash coming into the game is placed.

Double Odds — in some casinos they permit a player to take an Odds bet at twice his original stake on the line.

easy way — the numbers 4, 6, 8, 10 being rolled in a way other than with doubles, e.g., 4 rolled with a 3 and 1, instead of 2 and 2.

ee-yo — slang for 11.

even money — odds of 1 to 1. A dollar won for each dollar bet.

Field bet — a bet that 2, 3, 4, 9, 10, 11, 12 will be the next roll of the dice. Some layouts use a 5 instead of a 9, and some pay double or triple on either 2 or 12.

Free bets — taking Odds is referred to as a Free bet, because the casino has no advantage on Odds bets.

floorman — supervisor of the gaming tables.

Front Line — same as Pass Line.

full-odds — the correct odds as an Odds bet.

get out — to be loser and get even.

hand — the lapsed time and rolls of one shooter from the come-out to miss-out.

Hard-way — the numbers 4, 6, 8, 10 made with a pair. As 8 with two 4's.

Hop bets — a one-roll bet that the next roll or "hop" of the dice will be a specific number combination. This bet must be made to the Boxman, as it doesn't appear on the layout.

Horn bets — a one-roll proposition bet which is a combination of Any Crap (2, 3, or 12) and a bet on the 11. It must be wagered in multiples of four times the table minimum. It pays off according to the individual payoff of each number less the 3 chips that were lost.

Horn High bet — similar to a Horn bet, except one bets 5 units, specifying 2 units on any specific number (2, 3, 11, or 12).

"hot" hand — a succession of Passes.

Lay bet — a bet made on a point number that a 7 will be rolled before the point number. 5% commission.

layout — the game roadmap. The cloth on which the game is played.

limit — the maximum or minimum amount that can be wagered by one person.

long hand — describes a shooter's roll where many numbers are thrown before a point or seven-out brings the hand to a decision.

marker — an I.O.U.

miss-out — loser. Not making the point.

Natural — 7 or 11 on the come-out roll.

odds — the stipulated pay-off in wagering. When odds are correct, neither side has an advantage.

Odds bet — an additional bet that can be made by persons having Pass, Come, Don't Pass, or Don't Come bets. Paid at correct odds.

off numbers — the box numbers (4, 5, 6, 8, 9, 10). Generally, all point numbers except the shooter's.

one-roll bet — a bet decided on the next roll; as the Field, 7, 11, or Any Craps.

parlay — a system of betting. After a win the whole amount is wagered again.

Pass — a winning decision for Pass Line bettors.

Pass Line — a bet on the Pass Line is a bet that the shooter wins.

percentage — in gambling, the hidden or direct charge made by the casino.

pit — the ring of Craps tables.

pit boss — floorman; supervisor of the gaming tables.

Place bet — a bet made on a box number that the number will be rolled before a 7.

player — gambler, a bettor.

punter — player, bettor (England)

point — any of the numbers 4, 5, 6, 8, 9, 10 when rolled on the come-out roll.

point numbers — all the box numbers 4, 5, 6, 8, 9, 10.

press — increase the size of the next bet.

probability — the chance that one particular event out of many will happen.

proposition bet — bets on 11, 12, Hard-ways, 2, 3, 7, etc.; the long shots.

push — a standoff.

"right" bettor — person betting the dice will win. Pass Line bettor.

seven-out — indicates shooter has thrown a 7 and lost after establishing a point. Pass Line loses; Don't Pass wins; a Come bet wins, a Don't Come loses.

shill — starter. Person employed by the casino to act as a player to start the games.

shooter — the person in possession of the dice.

Single Odds — see *Odds bet*.

sleeper — a winning bet forgotten by the player.

GLOSSARY

standoff — no action. With a roll of 12 on the come-out for the Don't Pass, a tie.

stick — device that looks somewhat like a hockey stick which the Stickman uses to move the dice back to the shooter.

Stickman — the dealer (croupier) who calls the game and controls the pace.

system — any advance play of money management in a gambling game.

table limit — smallest and largest bet allowed at the table.

three-way Craps — a bet on 2, 3, and 12.

token or **toke** — tip. The gratuity given dealers.

unit — any fixed quantity when used in describing types of bets or systems.

vigorish — house percentage. (Vig.)

Whirl bet — a seldom used wager on all five of the come-out decision numbers (2, 3, 7, 11, and 12).

working bets — all the money or checks (chips) on the layout awaiting a decision.

"wrong" bettor — person betting the dice lose. Don't Pass Line bettor.

INDEX

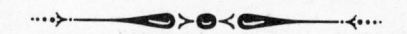

INDEX